What do I want to be for Halloween this year?

I0489601

How I'll design my jack-o-lantern

Favorite place in the neighborhood to stop during trick-or-treating

"I got a rock" - worst Halloween treats

The most uncomfortable costume I ever had

What makes a good costume

What would happen if I got stuck in my costume and turned into a _____?

The scariest story I ever heard

If I were Frankenstein's creator, what would I have made him look like?

Going through a haunted mansion

Stuck in a corn maze

Write a story about seeing a black cat on Halloween

My favorite costume ever

The greatest scary movie of all time

Picking out a pumpkin from the pumpkin patch

What will you use to collect all of your treats?

A thunderstorm on Halloween

Drinking the witch's brew

What would happen if you saw someone wearing the same costume?

The origins of Halloween

The best costume I ever saw

Who am I going trick-or-treating with this year?

My family's Halloween traditions

Best trick-or-treating weather

Spiders and creepy-crawly things

What if I discovered my house was haunted?

Bats in the belfry (bell tower) ...

What I like (or don't like) about Halloween

The spookiest ghost story ever

Tricks and treats on Halloween

Spending the night in a graveyard

What if your Halloween costume came to life and chased you?

If I could cast a spell, what would it be?

The best Halloween decorations

Legends of the haunted house

What is the best treat to get on Halloween?

What if you went to a school for ghosts?

Who carves the pumpkin in your house, and why?

The most popular Halloween costume

Imagine your dinner companion turned out to be a vampire?

What if your dad was a warlock?

Would you rather eat worms or spiders as a Halloween trick?

Belinda the black cat

When the skeleton in the biology room came to life

Finding out your older brother is a werewolf

Does your family ever dress up in costumes that match each other?

How old will I be when I stop trick-or-treating?

The Great Pumpkin

Who would win in a fight between a werewolf and a vampire?

What would you like your teacher to dress up as for Halloween?

Solving a Halloween mystery with Scooby Doo and the Mystery Machine

The tradition of All Soul's Day

Going horseback-riding with the headless horseman

The scariest looking house in my neighborhood

Bobbing for apples

The best thing about the school Halloween party

A day in the life of a ghost

How to prepare for a zombie attack

The year my sister's dolls came to life

If I were a wizard, what would I do?

Scariest Halloween legends

A ghost in my house that can walk through walls

Sneaking on board a pirate ship

If I had a flying broom, where would I go?

A pumpkin house

The best flavor of candy corn

Getting lost in a dark forest

What if your best friend turned into a zombie?

Finding a bat in your backpack

Funny Halloween jokes

Having a jack-o-lantern for a head

The night of the full moon

Best scary mystery books

What if your mother was a mummy?

What if you wake up as an imaginary creature, like a vamp-wolf,
or a skele-ummy

What would you create if you were a mad scientist?

Dracula visits the dentist

When gummy worms come to life

I got an eerie feeling when I heard...

The mysterious object started floating in the air and...

The Halloween pumpkin turned into a...

The black cat started to crouch and hiss when...

Something in the closet was making a strange noise, so I opened the door and...

The white sheets with black eyes peering through holes of the costume gave no clue as to who the kid was...

I couldn't believe my eyes when I saw...

You won't believe this story, but it is true...

If I had a flying broom, where would I go?

A pumpkin house

The best flavor of candy corn

Getting lost in a dark forest

What if your best friend turned into a zombie?

Finding a bat in your backpack

Funny Halloween jokes

Having a jack-o-lantern for a head

The night of the full moon

_____

_____

_____

_____

_____

_____

_____

Best scary mystery books

What if your mother was a mummy?

What if you wake up as an imaginary creature, like a vamp-wolf, or a skele-ummy

What would you create if you were a mad scientist?

Dracula visits the dentist

When gummy worms come to life

What if you went to a school for ghosts?

Who carves the pumpkin in your house, and why?

The most popular Halloween costume

Imagine your dinner companion turned out to be a vampire?

What if your dad was a warlock?

What is the scariest thing that has ever happened to you? Why was it so scary?

Pretend the mayor of your town wants to outlaw Halloween.
Write a letter to convince him that this is not a good idea.

What was the best Halloween costume you have ever had? What made it so special?

Pretend you are in charge of your class Halloween party. Make a plan for what you will do. What games will you play? What food will you eat?

If you could only do one, would you rather go to a Halloween party or go trick-or-treating? Why?

Do you like reading scary books or going to scary movies? Why or why not?

Write a Halloween acrostic poem using one of these words:
Halloween, Monster, Ghost, Vampire, Zombie.

Write a Halloween story using as many onomatopoeias such as "crackle," "squish" and "plop."

Explain Halloween to someone from another country where Halloween is not celebrated.

Create a list of safety rules for Trick-or-Treating.

What is something that used to scare you but no longer does?
Why was it so scary?

Write a story about visiting a haunted house.

Which Halloween monster (ghost, vampire, werewolf, zombie, mummy, etc.) do you think is the scariest? Why?

Pretend you are going to interview a vampire. Write ten
questions you would ask him or her.

Some schools have replaced Halloween with a Harvest Festival.
Do you think this is a good or a bad idea? Why?

You and your friends have created a haunted house. Make a flyer to tell people about it and convince them to come and visit.

Would you spend a night in a graveyard for $100? Why or why not?

Write a story from a Jack-O-Lantern's point of view.

Finish this sentence: This Halloween, I hope...

You're a mad scientist. Today in your lad you are creating a new monster. Can you describe this monster?

Write a spooky story about three ghosts to tell around the campfire. Don't forget to end on a big finale to scare everyone!

One night, after carving a pumpkin its start speaking to you.

You hear a strange sound from your wardrobe, you open it and see...

A bat flies into your room and says he needs your help.

Describe your perfect haunted house and draw a picture

What is the scariest thing you ever seen? And are you still scared of it?

You find some footprints leading in your house. What do you do?

Your imaginary friend becomes real and starts causing trouble for you.

Write 10 questions to interview a vampire and answer them from the point of view of a vampire

Write a recipe for a witch's brew.

Write three acrostic poems using the words, Halloween, witch and Frankenstein.

If I were a superhero, I would be...

Suppose aliens abducted you as you were walking to school.
Write a story telling about this experience.

Write about having wings and what you would do.

If I were on a deserted island I would...

You are the last surviving member of the human race. What do you do?

Imagine that you could be invisible for one day. Write a story about that day.

Soon you will met a genie and be granted 3 wishes. What would they be? Why?